Banking on Mergers:

Financial Power versus the Public Interest

Murray Cooke

Centre for Social Justice
Toronto

Correspondence to: Murray Cooke <mcooke@yorku.ca>

Library and Archives Canada Cataloguing in Publication
Cooke, Murray, 1970-

Banking on mergers : financial power versus the public interest / Murray Cooke.
Includes bibliographical references.

ISBN 0-9733292-5-4
1. Bank mergers--Canada. 2. Banks and banking--Canada. 3. Financial services industry--Canada. 4. Financial services industry--Government policy--Canada. 5. Corporate power--Canada. 6. Social responsibility of business--Canada. I. Centre for Social Justice II. Title.

HG2704.C67 2005 332.1'0971 C2005-907645-3

Published by Centre for Social Justice
489 College Street, Suite 303, Toronto, ON M6G 1A5
Ph: 416-927-0777 Toll Free: 1-888-803-8881
Fax: 416-927-7771
Email: justice@socialjustice.org
www.socialjustice.org

Date of publication – 2006
Printed and bound in Canada by union labour

Layout and Cover Design:
Visualeyez CREATIVE • Alan Pinn
Email: alanpinn@cogeco.ca • 705.741.4729

Table of Contents

Introduction and Overview 1

Canada's Financial Giants:
Corporate Connections and Corporate Power 6

Nuturing The Banks:
Public Regulation of the Financial Sector 14

Market Liberalization and Regulatory Reform:
From Banks to Financial Groups 17

Merger Mania:
Canadians say 'No' - Paul Martin says 'Not Yet' 25

The Canadian Financial Services Sector Today:
Transnational Financial Groups 28

Conclusion:
'Better Banks, Not Bigger Banks' 49

Works Cited 54

Endnotes 62

Acknowledgements:

Thanks to David Langille, John Peters, Dennis Pilon, Ewa Cerda-Llanos, Alex Montgomery-Robb, and Anna Poliszot for their editorial assistance and to Leo Panitch for his comments on an earlier version of this paper. Thanks to the organizers of the York Political Economy Student Conference held at York University in May 2003 and the discussant for my paper, Greg Albo, who helped develop the idea for this publication. Thanks as well to the financial institutions for providing photographs.

INTRODUCTION AND OVERVIEW

"Perhaps nowhere in the world can be found so intensive a degree of close organization as among bank interests in Canada."

Gustavus Myers,
A History of Canadian Wealth, 1914.

"By any standard, Canada already has one of the most concentrated banking systems in the world."

Paul Martin, Finance Minister,
Statement on bank mergers
December 14, 1998.

Listening to the CEOs of Canada's largest banks talk about bank mergers, one quickly gathers that they perceive themselves to be victims of political persecution. We are told that the poor banks, being unable to merge, are doomed to global irrelevance and threatened by foreign competition and ultimately by foreign takeovers. The bankers' cause has been championed by the business press that portrays the federal government as foolishly attempting to delay the inevitable and beneficial consolidation of the domestic banking sector. The bankers and most financial reporters are united in denouncing the federal government's reluctance to approve bank mergers as political interference obstructing good business sense.

Yet, the notion of the banks as victims seems rather far-fetched – especially when they announce their financial results. Similarly, the description of successive federal governments as anti-bank rings rather hollow when one looks at the changing regulatory environment for the financial sector. Financial deregulation by the federal government since the 1980s has allowed the banks to diversify and expand their financial activities. The Canadian financial services sector is no longer divided into distinct pillars characterized by specific financial institutions and their core business activities, namely banks, insurance companies, brokerage firms and trusts.[1] In this liberalized environment, the banks have diversified and taken over many domestic firms. Entire sections of Canada's financial industry, in particular the independent brokerage firms and trusts, have virtually disappeared in the face of the banking offensive. The marketplace is now dominated by a small number of large, diversified financial conglomerates functioning on a transnational scale.

Successive Canadian governments have facilitated and encouraged this growth and consolidation. At the same time, public policy at all levels has closely followed the recommendations of the major banks and the rest of the corporate elite. From the overall focus on balanced budgets and international competitiveness to specific policies such as cuts to the capital gains tax and the removal of the foreign content regulations on pension investments, the federal government's embrace of neo-liberalism has greatly benefited Canada's big banks.

The big banks' displeasure over the lack of an unequivocal green light for mergers should not be isolated from this larger context of bank and business-friendly policies. Still, it is notable that the banks have not been able to get their way in terms of further mergers and consolidation in the banking sector. In 1998, the federal government blocked two major bank mergers. Since that time, the banks have waited for a positive signal from government to re-launch the merger process. Much to the chagrin of the banks, the federal government has repeatedly engaged in consultations, conducted studies and produced reports on the topic, but has remained publicly ambivalent about the idea of mergers.

Having diversified their business activities, there is little room left for the big banks to grow in Canada. Tired of competing for market share, the big banks hope to grow through teaming up with each other through mergers. Even more important to the big Canadian banks are the opportunities offered by foreign markets, especially in the US. Unlike Canada, the US has many mid-sized and small state and local banks. As consolidation proceeds in the US, the Canadian banks would like to expand their presence in the huge US market by acquiring some of these smaller US firms. To expand abroad and to make foreign acquisitions, the Canadian banks argue that they must consolidate and gain size in their home market. Focused on foreign expansion, the Canadian banks have fostered a trend toward international liberalization. In order to gain access to foreign markets through bilateral and multilateral trade negotiations, the Canadian state must facilitate increased foreign access to the Canadian market. Canada's big banks will happily concede foreign access to the domestic market in which their dominant position is well entrenched, in order to gain access to larger foreign markets. The Canadian banks then conveniently turn around and argue that the foreign 'threat' requires further domestic consolidation.

To expand abroad and to make foreign acquisitions, the Canadian banks argue that they must consolidate and gain size in their home market.

However, none of this is inevitable or, from the perspective of the Canadian public, desirable. The federal government retains the discretion to approve or block large bank mergers. Bank mergers have not been ruled out but the federal government continues to state that mergers must be judged to be in the public interest in order to be permitted. Issues such as customer service, branch closures, job losses, conflicts of interest and the concentration of corporate power remain at the forefront of public concerns. Canada's banking sector is already highly concentrated. Mergers would lead to further concentration of banking assets and financial power. The merged banks would rationalize their branch networks and lay off employees. Canadian borrowers and consumers of other financial services would have fewer options to choose from.

Canada's business sector remains divided over the desirability of bank mergers. The leadership of the small business community, while solidly right-wing and highly supportive of free market policies, is very skeptical about bank mergers. Small business owners are wary of increased corporate concentration and fewer avenues of financing. Even corporate Canada appears less than enthusiastic about bank mergers. Some non-bank financial institutions fear the increased power that would result from bank mergers. Other financial institutions, including some of the smaller banks and credit unions, support bank mergers knowing that they could pick up business from customers left behind by the newly merged banks.

The business case for mergers is not clear cut. Many large business mergers result in problems. Among large financial institutions, the international experience with mergers is mixed. There is insufficient evidence to prove that banks must become global giants to gain efficiency and there have been large global banks that have struggled. A merged bank that ran into financial difficulties would create great instability for the Canadian market, the Canadian government and ultimately all Canadians as consumers and taxpayers. The Canadian banks have previously encountered turbulence in their foreign operations. If a merged Canadian bank were to rapidly expand abroad, the risk of domestic turmoil due to foreign market troubles would be magnified.

Donald Stewart,
CEO, Sun Life Financial

Over the last couple of years a new wrinkle has been added to the debate over bank mergers. The largest life insurance firms, also beneficiaries of market liberalization, have emerged as potential merger partners for the banks. While the banks are in favour of allowing such mergers, the life insurance firms are divided over this issue. Many of the same issues would be raised in a bank-insurance merger as in a mega-bank merger, such as increased financial concentration and corporate power. Issues such as bank branch closures would be less of a concern, though presumably many local insurance brokers would be hurt. Other issues, such as the increased pressure on consumers to obtain all their financial services from one firm and concerns about the use of consumer information, would emerge.

Any future proposals for mergers among Canada's biggest financial institutions must be evaluated in light of the larger public interest. To determine the public interest, open public hearings and broad consultations must be held. Various constituencies, including marginalized groups, rural communities and small business must be heard from.

The decision to approve or reject bank mergers should not be left to the federal government's Competition Bureau nor to the financial regulators in the Office of the Superintendent of Financial Institutions. Furthermore the Finance Minister must retain the discretion to judge any proposals based on input from parliamentarians and the public. The banks and their media allies portray this as 'political interference' and would prefer that the government show 'leadership' by ignoring public opinion, but this minimal level of democratic accountability should be strengthened not abandoned. Any attempt to restrict debate or limit public consultations must be resisted.

Simply debating for or against mergers is much too narrow of a discussion. Beyond merger proposals, the discussion of the financial sector should include a broader debate about corporate accountability and democratic control. Even without mergers, the status quo involves insufficient protection for consumers, excess corporate concentration, and a complete lack of democratic control and corporate accountability. Through their allocation of financial resources, the major financial institutions hold an enormous amount of power over the economy and our lives. Reigning in financial power, subordinating it to national and local control, and redirecting it toward productive and socially useful investments is the larger project that we must begin to tackle.

CANADA'S FINANCIAL GIANTS: CORPORATE CONNECTIONS AND CORPORATE POWER

"The political power of the larger banks and of the Bankers' Association can hardly be exaggerated. The bank acts were written largely by the very banks supposedly regulated by them."

Tom Naylor
The History of Canadian Business 1867-1914, 1975.

"It has always been informal...If anyone had any views they wanted to express then they request a meeting...It is not unusual for guys to get together."

David Moorcroft, RBC spokesperson,
on bank CEOs meeting with the Finance Minister.
Globe and Mail, August 24, 2004.

Canada's major financial services firms are among the largest corporations in the country. Through growth and mergers, the large life insurance companies have joined the big banks in the first tier of Canada's financial elite, rivaling the big banks in size. With five major banks and three large life insurance firms, Canada now has eight large diversified financial groups (see Table 1).

Canada's major financial institutions have always been central to the country's corporate elite and cozy with the political elite. The boards of the major financial corporations are a meeting place for the corporate and political elite in Canada. Back in the 1880s, Canada Life scored the ultimate coup when the current Prime Minister John A. Macdonald served as company president. Similarly, John Abbott served as a director of the Bank of Montreal while Prime Minister. In fact, the first three Ministers of Finance after Confederation were all closely connected to a chartered bank (MacIntosh, 1991: 14-15).

For the sake of discretion, it became seen as more appropriate for leading political figures to serve on corporate boards before or after, rather than during, their political careers. Alexander Mackenzie, Mackenzie Bowell, Charles Tupper and Robert Borden all went on to become presidents of life insurance companies after their tenures as Prime Minister (McQueen, 1985: 8). Prime Ministers Robert Borden and R.B. Bennett became directors of Scotiabank and the Royal Bank respectively.

Table 1: Canada's Major Banks and Life Insurance Companies Ranked by Annual Profit, 2004
($ billions)

	Market Value[1]	Total Assets[2]	Annual Revenues[2]	Annual Profits[2]
Bank of Nova Scotia	40.35	279.21	10.46	2.93
Royal Bank	43.33	429.20	17.35	2.87
Manulife Financial	46.59	184.25	27.15	2.56
Bank of Montreal	28.08	265.19	9.61	2.35
TD Bank	33.04	311.03	10.83	2.31
CIBC	24.40	278.76	11.88	2.20
Sun Life Financial	23.60	107.76	21.75	1.68
Great-West Lifeco	25.83	95.85	21.74	1.66
National Bank	8.59	88.81	3.55	0.73

1. As of February 22, 2005.
2. As of October 31, 2004 for the banks and December 31, 2004 for the insurance companies.

Sources: Toronto Stock Exchange; Canadian Bankers Association, *Database of Domestic Banks' Financial Results*; Annual Corporate Reports.

This cozy relationship between the public sector and top corporate boards continues into the 21st century. Financial company boards currently feature a smattering of former federal cabinet ministers (Michael Wilson of Manulife, Don Mazankowski of Great-West Life, Barbara McDougall of Scotiabank and John Manley of CIBC), an influential Liberal senator (Michael Kirby of Scotiabank), a former Premier (Daniel Johnson of Great-West Life), two directors of the Canada Pension Plan Investment Board (Gail Cook-Bennett of Manulife and Helen Sinclair of TD), a former governor of the Bank of Canada (Gordon Thiessen of Manulife) and a former American ambassador to Canada (Gordon Giffin of CIBC). Brian Mulroney was briefly a director of CIBC before he became Prime Minister. Jean Chrétien served on the board of Toronto-Dominion during his sabbatical from active politics during the 1980s. Just as former Liberal Premier of New Brunswick Frank McKenna resigned from the board of BMO in early 2005 to take up the post of Canadian ambassador to the US, former Deputy Prime Minister and Finance Minister John Manley joined the board of CIBC to maintain his Bay Street ties while bidding his time before another run at the Liberal Party leadership and the Prime Minister's Office.

Few corporations are as closely connected to the corridors of political power as Power Corporation, the parent company of Great-West Life and IGM Financial, the largest mutual fund company in the country. Prime Ministers Trudeau, Mulroney, Chrétien and Martin have all had business and/or personal ties to Power Corporation and its chairperson Paul Desmarais, currently the 6th richest person in Canada (Newman, 1998: 165-189). Martin got his start at Canada Steamship Lines while it was owned by Power Corporation (Chodos et al., 1988). Mulroney currently sits on Power Corporation's International Advisory Council (Yakabuski, 2004).

The connections between the major financial firms and the rest of the corporate sector in Canada have always been extensive. The boards of the leading Canadian banks have served as the central nodes of an elaborate system of interlocking directorships that connect the financial sector to the industrial sector and make up Canada's corporate elite. William Carroll's research (2004) has demonstrated that despite the internationalization of the economy and the restructuring of corporate governance, the ties between Canada's financial elite and other sectors of the Canadian corporate elite persist. The boards of Canada's major chartered banks remain an important meeting place for Canada's corporate elite and some of the richest individuals in the country (See Table 2). Along with the high-profile names such as Gerry Schwartz and Paul Sobey (both directors of Scotiabank), are perhaps less familiar names such as Brandt Louie (RBC), Charles Sirois (CIBC), John Bragg (TD) and Nancy Southern (Bank of Montreal) all of whom appear either individually or through their families on the list of the 100 richest Canadians (Canadian Business, 2004).[2]

Table 2: The Canadian Banks' Corporate Interlocks

Bank	Bank directors also serve as directors or executives of the following Canadian or foreign firms: (rank among largest Canadian corporations by revenues, 2003).
Bank of Montreal	George Weston Ltd (2), Onex (13), Nortel (20), Petro-Canada (23), Shell Canada (27), Husky Energy (31),* Hudson's Bay Company (33), TransCanada Corporation (50), Shoppers Drug Mart (61), Atco Ltd (68), Canadian Utilities Limited (subsidiary of Atco), Canadian Pacific Railway (72), Cascades Inc. (80), Tembec Inc. (93), CGI Group (100), Masonite International Corporation (115), Transcontinental Inc. (144), Norske Skog Canada Ltd (153), Torstar (177), Toromont Industries Ltd. (195), Husky Injection Molding Ltd (204), AXA Assurance Inc. (212), Fairmont Hotels & Resorts (240), Reitmans Canada (266), First Service Corporation (271), CFM Corporation (314), GSW Inc. (384), Goldcorp Inc. (457), PrimeWest Energy (477), Inmet Mining Corporation (498). Other notable links: Foreign: Altran Technologies, Cheung Kong Infrastructure Holdings Ltd,* CK Life Sciences International,* E.W. Scripps Company. [*These firms are part of the business empire of Hong Kong billionaire Li Ka-Shing and family]
Bank of Nova Scotia	Decoma International Inc. (subsidiary of Magna International 5), BCE Inc. (9), Onex (13), Celestica Inc. (subsidiary of Onex), Petro-Canada (23), Empire Co. (26), Sobeys Inc. (subsidiary of Empire Co.), Inco (78), Cascades Inc. (80), Stelco (96), Gerdau Ameristeel Corporation (103), Imperial Tobacco Canada (140), MDS Inc. (156), Extendicare Inc. (160), Emera Inc. (203), Nova Scotia Power Incorporated (subsidiary of Emera Inc.), Wajax Ltd (258), Manitoba Telecom Services (269), MDC Partners Inc. (286), Indigo Books and Music (287), Independent Order of Foresters (305), CFM Corporation (314). Other notable links: Foreign: Amatil Investments (Singapore) Ltd, Blue Cross and Blue Shield of Florida, Rayovac Corporation, Wearnes International (1994) Ltd.
CIBC	Celestica Inc. (a subsidiary of Onex 13), Nortel (20), Telus (34), Canadian Tire (35), Noranda (36), Sears Canada (39), Canadian National Railway (43), Canadian Natural Resources Ltd (53), Tricap Restructuring Fund (a subsidiary of Brascan 60), Talisman Energy (63), Dofasco (75), ING Canada (90), TransAlta (113), CanWest Global (123), MDS Inc. (156), Linamar Corporation (171), Saskatchewan Wheat Pool (180), Telesystem Ltd. (the parent company of Telesystem International Wireless 186), CAE Inc. (217), Wajax Ltd (258), Western Forest Products Inc. (formerly Doman Industries Ltd 345). Other notable links: Canadian: Cadillac Fairview Corporation [owned by Ontario Teachers' Pension Plan]. Foreign: Bowater Incorporated, Brunswick Corporation, E.W. Scripps Company, Federated Department Stores, Inc., PepsiCo.

Royal Bank	BCE Inc. (9), Bell Globemedia Inc. (subsidiary of BCE), Aliant Inc. (subsidiary of BCE), Imperial Oil (10), EnCana Corporation (18), Thomson Corporation (25), McCain Foods (37), Suncor Energy (38), Metro Inc. (46), TransCanada Corporation (50), Hydro One (66), Inco (78), SNC-Lavalin Group (85), Molson Inc. (112), TransAlta Corporation (113), McDonald's Canada (119), Canfor Corporation (129), Fairmont Hotels & Resorts (240), Rothmans (351), Astral Media (400). Other notable links: Canadian: H.Y. Louie Co., London Drugs Limited, IGA Canada Limited. Foreign: Coca-Cola, Dow Chemicals, IBM.
Toronto-Dominion Bank	Imperial Oil (10), Petro-Canada (23), Thomson Corporation (25), Empire Co. (26), Sobeys Inc. (subsidiary of Empire Co. 26), Telus (34), Sears Canada (39), Canadian National Railway Company (43), Metro Inc. (46), TransCanada Corporation (50), Canada Bread Ltd (subsidiary of Maple Leaf Foods 54), McCain Capital Corporation (largest shareholder of Maple Leaf Foods), Canadian Pacific Railway (72), Dofasco (75), Inco (78), SNC-Lavalin Group (85), Barrick Gold Corporation (94), Epcor Utilities (107), Teck Cominco Ltd (117), Transat A.T. Inc. (128), MDS Inc. (156), West Fraser Timber Co. (174), Harlequin Enterprises (subsidiary of Torstar 177). Other notable links: Foreign: Alpha Capital Fund, American International Group, Cleveland-Cliffs Inc, Collins & Aikman Corporation, eFunds Corporation, Lafarge North America, Lance, Inc., Mosaic Company, Premcor Inc., Roper Industries, Inc., Royal Philips Electronics, UnumProvident Corporation, WellPoint, Inc.

Source: Bank notices of Annual Meetings and Proxy Circulars, 2005; National Post Business Magazine. *FP500: Canada's Largest Corporations*. June 2004.

The concentration of the banking sector has facilitated close cooperation amongst the main players and strengthened their political influence. The Canadian Bankers Association (CBA) dates back to 1891 and has traditionally promoted cooperation over competition within the banking sector (Darroch, 1994: 87, 253). The CBA has attempted, not always successfully, to give the banking sector a unified voice in discussions with government over regulatory issues. As some of Canada's largest corporations they play an influential role in building the corporate consensus on public policy issues and framing the political debate through organizations such as the Canadian Council of Chief Executives (formerly the Business Council on National Issues).

The big banks and insurance companies were among Canada's earliest and most important transnational corporations. Canada's major banks operated internationally almost from their beginnings in order to finance trade and gain access to foreign capital markets (Darroch, 1994: 251-252). Considering Canada's economic relations, it is not surprising that Canadian banks established agencies and branches in both Britain and the US. Today, Scotiabank is the most international of Canada's banks with operations in some 50 countries. From its beginning in 1832, the Bank of Nova Scotia had ties with the West Indies and it continues to be the leading bank in the Caribbean and Central America with operations in 25 countries within the region (Darroch, 1994: 81, 85; Waugh, 2004). A recent focus has been on Mexico, where Scotiabank Inverlat is the seventh largest bank in the country. In terms of their international presence, the insurance companies have not been left behind. Business historian Michael Bliss wrote that "In the 1890s Canadian life insurance salesmen travelled the world, opening new markets for their policies, importing capital to Canada where their companies could invest it profitably" (1987: 270). Today, the life insurance companies are extremely active in foreign markets. In 2003, foreign premium income accounted for 54 percent of Canadian life insurance company premiums, up from 37 percent in 1990 (CLHIA, 2005; Finance, 2002).

The big banks and insurance companies were among Canada's earliest and most important transnational corporations

During the postwar period Canada's financial sector was lucrative but rather sleepy and conservative. On the domestic front, individual sectors of the financial services industry tended to operate as relatively non-competitive oligarchies. Internationally, the postwar order was designed to facilitate trade but sought to restrict international capital flows. At the beginning of the 1960s, the Canadian banks' international activities were focused on retail banking through their foreign branches particularly in the UK, US and the Caribbean (Nagy, 1983). However, since the late 1960s international financial markets have undergone a major transformation.

The rise (or re-emergence) of international investment flows and increased opportunities for global banking reflected the growing strength of neo-liberal free market ideology and was facilitated by the decisions of the governments of the leading capitalist countries, particularly the United States (Helleiner, 1994). The Canadian banks expanded their international activities but they soon learned that along with new opportunities also came increased risks. The oil shocks of the 1970s led to huge bank deposits of petro-dollars that were recycled through loans to developing countries. The Third World debt crisis of the early 1980s precipitated by the introduction of high interest rates and the onset of recession generated major loan losses for the Canadian banks. An international banking crisis was avoided through the leadership of the US government and the international financial institutions, but the developing countries have yet to escape debt bondage. Canada's banks would get burned again when the late 1980s real estate boom collapsed.

Despite the risks and the financial crises that have periodically enveloped specific countries or regions, the internationalization of financial markets has continued to expand. Canada's banks have expanded their international activities but in global terms their size and importance has declined relative to other international banks. In 1970, three Canadian banks were among the twenty-five largest banks in the world ranked by assets. By the 1990s Canada's largest bank was ranked approximately fiftieth in the world (see Table 3). Reflecting their role as middle-players rather than global giants and the realities of the continental economy, by the 1990s the Canadian banks were shifting from global aspirations to a more focused emphasis on a North American continental strategy (Darroch, 1994, 1999).

Table 3: International Ranking of Canadian Banks, 1970-2003
(Position among the world's banks, ranked by assets)

	1970	1975	1980	1985	1990	1995	2000	2003
RBC	10	22	23	32	51	61	53	50
CIBC	13	29	36	46	58	62	58	62
BMO	25	45	50	40	76	72	63	66
Scotiabank	43	53	55	60	81	76	62	61
TD	56	66	71	75	113	100	59	63

Source: *The Banker*, various years.

The liberalization and expansion of financial markets around the world has increased the power of financial interests relative to governments, non-financial corporations and communities. It is important to remember, as American business observer Doug Henwood reminds us, that:

> *financial claims confer real authority on their owners. Stockholders have demanded steadily higher profits, which kept corporations downsizing and outsourcing even in the best times. Bondholders have pressured state and local governments to trim their budgets. Bankers and bondholders (in alliance with state institutions like the IMF) have forced severe economic restructuring on debtor countries (2003: 203).*

The cutthroat discipline imposed by the strength of financial interests has been one of the strengths of the American model of shareholder capitalism in terms of its ability to generate corporate profitability (Seccombe, 2000: 132). Shareholders, including powerful institutional investors such as pension funds and mutual funds, push corporate managers to ruthlessly focus on short-term stock valuations. The downside of this rampant financial power can be seen in the attack on progressive taxation, social programs, social infrastructure, employment standards and workers' rights. The banks themselves have been remarkably successful in keeping unions out. Despite past organizing drives, most notably in the 1970s, Canada's big banks remain as non-unionized as Wal-Mart or McDonald's.[3] While Canada's powerful corporate elite has successfully pushed governments at all levels to adopt the neo-liberal corporate agenda, Canadians have seen a growing gap between the rich and the poor, increased poverty and homelessness and increased economic insecurity.

NURTURING THE BANKS:
PUBLIC REGULATION OF THE FINANCIAL SECTOR

"In Canada, public policy has deliberately aimed at facilitating the development of strong, large banks with national reach."

Task Force on the Future of the Canadian Financial Services Sector, Final Report, September 1998.

"Far from being a straitjacket, government regulation has provided our banks fertile ground to grow and flourish, not only within our own borders but also around the world."

Paul Martin, Finance Minister,
December 14, 1998.

Much of the debate about 'globalization' has assumed a withering away of the state in the face of global market forces and a nascent transnational governance structure. This seriously misrepresents the extent to which globalization has been facilitated and driven by state actions. The misunderstanding has been driven by the rhetoric of neo-liberalism. Contrary to what neo-liberalism might seem to suggest, a strong and able state is necessary to sustain a free-market economy.

While the deregulation of financial services has been a common theme since the 1980s, the Canadian state retains a prominent role in shaping and supporting the financial services sector. Though the state has liberalized market activities, significant restrictions remain on business powers, forms of corporate organization and patterns of ownership. Regulatory structures have been consolidated and their mandates and roles formalized to respond to a more competitive marketplace. The state continues to play a vital role in providing consumer protection, ensuring prudential stability and acting as lender of last resort. Finance Minister Paul Martin's rejection of two huge bank mergers in December 1998 was an obvious example of the continuing relevance of the state. The Canadian state's role in the financial services sector serves as a reminder that globalization cannot be equated with the withering away of the state.

Traditionally, Canadian regulators have favoured safety and soundness over competition in the financial sector. Domestic firms were protected from foreign competition and oligarchies of large national firms were encouraged. According to business professor James Darroch, "the role of government regulation in encouraging a concentrated and Canadian-owned industry has been critical" (1994: 5). By the 1920s, Canada's banking regulations had facilitated the emergence of a small number of large banks with national networks of bank branches.

Canada's financial services sector was segmented into four pillars: banks, trusts, insurance companies and securities dealers. Until the 1950s, the core functions performed by each pillar remained quite separate and distinct. The main reasons for separation were to ensure stability and to avoid conflicts of interest. For example, a bank that was providing loans to a given firm and underwriting and selling that firm's securities would face a potential conflict of interest.

In the 1950s and 1960s, amid foreign encroachments into Canada, the federal government acted to ensure a Canadian-controlled financial services sector. In 1957, the federal government passed legislation that facilitated the conversion of the largest stock life insurance companies into mutual companies owned by their policyholders. A number of major firms, including Canada Life, Manulife and Sun Life, took this route, which provided protection against foreign takeover. In 1964, Finance Minister Walter Gordon announced measures to protect domestic financial firms, including banks, life insurance companies and trusts from foreign takeover. New York based Citibank had already ignored the wishes of the Canadian government and purchased the small Mercantile Bank. The Chase Manhattan Bank was interested in gaining control of TD. Revisions to the Bank Act, put in place in 1967, prohibited foreign banks from operating branches or subsidiaries in Canada. Foreign interests could not collectively obtain more than 25 percent of the shares of an existing federally incorporated financial firm and individual foreign interests were limited to a 10 percent share.

Dominic D'Alessandro
CEO, Manulife Financial

Furthermore, the banks were required to be widely held. The maximum 10 percent share rule would apply to Canadians as well. Requiring banks to be widely held helps ensure the separation of financial and commercial activity and prevents the possibility of questionable self-dealing between a financial institution and its major shareholders. While the provisions limiting foreign ownership were phased out by the Canada-US Free Trade Agreement, NAFTA and GATT, as discussed below, the banks are still required to be widely held.

MARKET LIBERALIZATION AND REGULATORY REFORM: FROM BANKS TO FINANCIAL GROUPS

"There are no trust companies left today, there are no investment dealers of any real size, other than one or two of us. The next thing is insurance. That is the issue"

Michael Greenwood, President of Canaccord Capital,
Speaking to the Senate Banking Committee,
November 27, 2003.

"BMO Financial Group does not even sound like a bank any more. It used to be the Bank of Montreal, correct?...BMO sounds like a bad deodorant."

Frank Mahovlich, Senator and Member of the Hockey Hall of Fame, questioning Tony Comper, Chair and CEO of BMO, before the Senate Banking Committee
November 27, 2003.

A notable feature of Canada's banking law has been the inclusion of a 'sunset' clause in the Bank Act leading to a periodic reassessment and updating of banking legislation.[4] This gives interested parties, such as the Canadian Bankers Association, a frequent opportunity to seek desired changes to the legislation. Since the early 1980s, the regulatory regime for financial services has been under almost constant review. Major reform packages were enacted in 1987, 1992 and 2001, plus the Task Force on the Future of the Canadian Financial Services Sector (the MacKay Task Force)[5] issued its report in 1998 following nearly two years of work.

Since at least 1987, a principal goal of these periodic reviews has been to increase competition in the financial services sector. This has been done in two ways: by encouraging greater competition between the existing players and by facilitating the entry of new players, both foreign and domestic. As competition among the players has increased, the state has placed the different players under an increasingly unified regulatory regime to replace the distinct regulatory regimes of the former pillars. At the same time that the Canadian state has unleashed the financial services sector to encourage greater competition and to allow firms to perform a wider array of activities the state has engaged in a process of re-regulation within the sector. To regulate the highly competitive and innovative market, new regulatory agencies have been created, and others strengthened.

Allowing Foreign Banks and Breaking Down the Pillars

The first significant step in allowing new entrants to the Canadian financial services sector occurred in 1980 when foreign banks were permitted to establish banking subsidiaries in Canada. Foreign banks were legally able to enter Canada before 1967 but their impact remained insignificant. From 1967 to 1980, federal law prohibited foreign banks, though many foreign firms evaded the rules by incorporating non-bank financial institutions at the provincial level. After 1980, foreign banks could open subsidiaries in Canada, but a ceiling was placed on the size of the total foreign banking sector equal to 8 percent of total banking assets in Canada (Freedman, 1998: 8). The ceiling was raised to 16% in 1984 (MacIntosh, 1991: 179).

Changes introduced in 1987 and 1992 broke down the barriers between the different pillars of the domestic financial services sector.

Changes introduced in 1987 and 1992 broke down the barriers between the different pillars of the domestic financial services sector. As a first step in 1987, banks were permitted to own brokerage firms as subsidiaries. Then, in 1992 amendments to the Bank Act effectively ended the concept of the four pillars. Banks and insurance companies were allowed to own trust companies. Banks and trust and loan companies were permitted to own insurance companies, though they were restricted from marketing insurance through their branch networks. Widely held financial institutions, including insurance companies, would be permitted to establish a bank.

Complete market liberalization, however, has not yet been permitted. Since 1992, the banks have been lobbying hard to gain two business powers that remain outside their grasp: branch distribution of insurance and car leasing. Thus far, however, the insurance companies, auto manufacturers and auto dealers have successfully protected their turf.[6] The government has been caught in the middle of intense pressure from the banks seeking extended business powers and from non-bank financial institutions.

In 1992 as the pillars were dismantled, another major reform was introduced with little fanfare. Until that time, the chartered banks were required to hold reserves with the Bank of Canada. Reserves were intended to serve as protection against insolvency and allowed the central bank to influence the money supply by adjusting reserve levels. The banks had complained for years that reserves constituted an unfair 'tax' which placed them at a competitive disadvantage compared to other financial institutions. Bank reserves were quietly phased out over two years starting in 1992. This major concession to the banks was enacted by the Mulroney government with little public debate or awareness.

Having allowed foreign bank subsidiaries to be established in Canada in 1980, the federal government took further steps to open the financial services sector to foreign interests in the late 80s. The Canada-US Free Trade Agreement was groundbreaking in its inclusion of services, including financial services, in a trade liberalization agreement (White, 1997: 61). Through the FTA, US interests were excluded from the limits on foreign ownership of specific Canadian banks (the 25 percent rule) and foreign ownership of the Canadian banking sector as a whole (the 16 percent rule). As part of the North American Free Trade Agreement, Mexican interests were excluded from these limits as well. Through the Uruguay Round of GATT and the development of the General Agreement on Trades in Services (GATS), these limits were removed altogether in 1994 (Canada, 1998b: 103, 171).

Regulatory Reform: Can the State Still Regulate the Banks?

In 1987 as the pillars began to be dismantled, the Office of the Superintendent of Financial Institutions (OSFI) was created, consolidating the federal state's regulatory powers. Referring to the creation of OSFI, Michael Babad and Catherine Mulroney suggest that "one of the first concrete measures the Mulroney government took on the path to deregulation was actually reregulation" (1993: 33). The OSFI became responsible for overseeing all federally regulated financial institutions. At the same time, the Canada Deposit Insurance Corporation (CDIC) was strengthened and received a revised mandate and oversight powers.

Beyond restructuring the regulators, the groundbreaking 1987 and 1992 revisions to the financial institutions legislation have required a new regulatory approach. By allowing the pillars to merge, the state was forced to draw up new rules of proper business activity and behaviour. Previously, the separation of the pillars had served to reduce potential conflicts of interest and offer a degree of consumer protection. With expanded powers for financial institutions, the dangers have increased. Increased emphasis is now placed on legal rules of good governance, disclosure and transparency. New governance requirements were introduced in 1992, including "a requirement for one third of the directors to be unaffiliated, the creation of a conduct review committee and the imposition of a strict set of restrictions against self-dealing" (Canada, 1998a: 180).

Canadians should recognize that the state can still regulate the financial sector and that further steps toward market liberalization are not inevitable.

With financial institutions engaged in the full range of financial services and having access to large amounts of personal information, the need for a comprehensive consumer protection law has become more urgent. Consumer protection has been regulated through restrictions on the use of personal information by financial institutions, and provisions against coercive tied selling. Banks are not supposed to share customer information with their insurance or securities subsidiaries. This is intended to prevent banks from targeting particular customers for additional financial services based upon information gathered in a different context. The banks resent these restrictions on the use of information and the requirement that different services be offered through separate subsidiaries, because they restrict the benefits, such as economies of scale, gained through diversification. Coercive tied selling - making the provision of one service, such as a loan, conditional upon the use of another service - is a more direct abuse of power on the part of a financial institution. The 1997 Bank Act revisions included a section to prohibit coercive tied selling. This section, which was not proclaimed until September 30, 1998, makes it an offence to "impose undue pressure, or coerce, a person to obtain a product or service from…the bank and any of its affiliates, as a condition for obtaining a loan from the bank" (cited in Canada, 1998a: 133).

Réal Raymond, CEO
National Bank

These efforts to transform and increase regulatory oversight of the financial services sector in Canada, despite their weaknesses, belie any simplistic depiction of the withering away of the state in the face of globalization. In the words of Stephen Clarkson, "Canadian governments appear actually to have defied the putatively irreversible, state-shrinking logic of globalization and increased their regulatory and supervisory control over financial services" (2002: 157). Canadians should recognize that the state can still regulate the financial sector and that further steps toward market liberalization are not inevitable.

The Banks Become Diversified Financial Groups

The market openings offered by the reforms of 1987 and 1992 led to significant restructuring in the Canadian financial services sector (see Table 4). "Faced with pressure in most of their traditional business areas, Canada's banks responded like any other large corporation under attack: they bought out the competition." (Stanford, 1999: 57). Bank-owned brokerage firms became the dominant players in investment banking after 1987. The remaining independent (non-bank owned) investment dealers complained to the MacKay Task Force that regulatory reform had facilitated the emergence of a new banking "super-pillar" in place of the original four pillars (IID, 1997). In November 2002, Michael Greenwood of Canaccord Capital told the Senate Banking Committee that "the big six banks have approximately 86.4 percent of the full service and roughly 91.5 percent of the discount brokerage market. More importantly, the banks have more of the profitable business lines, such as fee-based accounts, which are the fastest growing in Canada" (Canada, 2002).

Table 4: The Collapsing Pillars

The Banks Takeover the Brokerage Firms

Bank of Montreal	acquired	Nesbitt Thomson	1987
Bank of Nova Scotia		McLeod Young Weir	1987
Royal Bank		Dominion Securities	1987
CIBC		Wood Gundy	1988

The Banks Takeover the Trusts

CIBC	acquired	Morgan Trust	1992
TD		Central Guaranty Trust	1992
Royal Bank		Royal Trust	1993
National Bank		General Trust	1993
Bank of Nova Scotia		Montreal Trust	1994
Bank of Nova Scotia		National Trust	1997
TD		Canada Trust	1999

In his comparative study of the financial services sector in Canada, France, Germany, the UK and the US, William Coleman argues that:

> *The economic and political changes of the past two decades have added to the economic power of domestically-owned commercial banks in Canada. They now dominate banking and securities markets to a greater extent than commercial banks in any of the other four countries. They own the largest securities houses, and they have become a major player in residential*

mortgages...Having taken over several large trust companies and having seen many others collapse, the banks face much weaker competition from these firms. Financial cooperatives continue to offer some competition, but only in Quebec might they be described as a significant force (1996: 224).

Since then, the absorption of the trusts by the banks continued. The Bank of Nova Scotia acquired National Trust in 1997 and TD acquired Canada Trust, the last remaining major independent trust, in 1999.

An important segment of the financial sector that was not one of the original pillars is the mutual funds industry. During the 1990s, this rapidly growing sector became a lucrative market for financial service institutions. The leading player in Canada's mutual fund business is IGM Financial which is controlled by Power Financial Corporation (see Table 5). The banks are heavily involved in this investment market. The wealth management subsidiaries of the five big banks rank among the eleven largest mutual fund companies in Canada. Together they managed approximately 35 percent of the mutual fund assets outstanding in January 2005, up from 25 percent at the end of 1997 (IFIC, 2005; Canada, 1998a: 46-47).

The life insurance companies also actively compete for the consumer investment market through mutual funds and segmented funds. Sun Life is the largest shareholder in CI Mutual Funds, a leading mutual fund company. Manulife Investments also makes the top twenty mutual fund firms. The banks and insurance companies do receive serious competition from foreign (AIM Trimark, Fidelity and Franklin Templeton) and independent Canadian (AGF) mutual fund companies. Foreign banks in Canada such as HSBC and ING manage relatively small mutual fund assets.

In the 1990s, Canadian financial institutions were allowed to develop into financial conglomerates offering a diverse range of services (Freedman, 1998: 15). Today, it seems hard to get the big banks to admit that they are 'banks.' Instead, the major banks and insurance companies accurately refer to themselves as diversified 'financial groups.'

Table 5: Largest Mutual Fund Companies
Mutual Fund Assets, January 2005
($ billions)

Rank	Company	Assets	Market Share
1	IGM Financial Inc.[1]	83.0	16.6%
2	**RBC Asset Management Inc.**	47.5	9.5%
3	C.I. Mutual Funds Inc.[2]	43.4	8.7%
4	AIM Trimark Investments	42.3	8.5%
5	**CIBC Asset Management**	42.2	8.4%
6	**TD Asset Management Inc.**	36.3	7.3%
7	Fidelity Investments Canada Limited	31.4	6.3%
8	AGF Management Limited	22.2	4.4%
9	Franklin Templeton Investments	20.2	4.0%
10	**BMO Investments Inc.**	19.9	4.0%
11	**Scotia Securities Inc.**	14.3	2.8%
12	Phillips Hager & North Ltd.	13.7	2.7%
13	Dynamic Mutual Funds	11.5	2.3%
14	MD Management Limited	10.7	2.1%
15	AIC Limited	10.6	2.1%
16	**National Bank Mutual Funds**	6.4	1.3%
17	Fiducie Desjardins	5.6	1.1%
18	Manulife Investments	5.4	1.1%
19	**Guardian Group of Funds Ltd.**[3]	4.7	--
20	Clarington Funds Inc.	3.8	--
21	**Altamira Investment Services Inc.**[4]	3.8	--
	Total big six banks	175.0	35.0%
	Industry total	500.4	100%

-- less than one percent
1. IGM Financial Inc., which is controlled by Power Financial Corporation, includes Investors Group, Mackenzie Financial Corporation and Counsel Wealth Management.
2. Sun Life Financial, with a 34% stake, is the largest shareholder in C.I. Fund Management Inc., the parent company of C.I. Mutual Funds Inc.
3. BMO acquired the Guardian Group of Funds Ltd in 2001.
4. The National Bank of Canada acquired Altamira in 2002.

Source: *The Investment Funds Institute of Canada.*

MERGER MANIA: CANADIANS SAY 'NO' – PAUL MARTIN SAYS 'NOT YET'

"Scotiabank's position is that these mergers must be analyzed very thoroughly, because from our viewpoint they represent bad public policy. This is bad for competition, bad for choice, bad for consumers in small business, bad in terms of potential concentration of risk and power, and it creates a concentration that is unhealthy in a country the size of Canada."

Peter Godsoe, Chair and CEO of Scotiabank
Speaking to the Senate Banking Committee,
October 7, 1998

"Bank mergers are about raising prices and reducing service to the public and concentrating economic power in the hands of the few. They may also be about the glorification of chief executives and the early cashing-in of stock options"

Doug Peters, former chief economist of TD bank
and former Secretary of State for International Financial Institutions,
Speaking to the House Finance Committee,
February 4, 2003

No other event in recent memory has demonstrated the continuing power and relevance of the Canadian state in the field of financial services like the Minster of Finance's refusal to allow two major bank mergers in late 1998. The proposed mergers were the subjects of intense public scrutiny for most of that year. The proceedings of the MacKay Task Force were shaken by the announcement on January 23, 1998 of the proposed merger of the Royal Bank and the Bank of Montreal, followed three months later by the TD - CIBC merger plan. These merger proposals were not and did not become part of the mandate of the task force. However, the task force recommended that mergers should not be rejected out of hand through the maintenance of a general policy of 'big shall not buy big.'

The banks worked feverishly to present the mergers as both desirable and inevitable. They argued that the mergers were necessary for them to compete and inevitable given global trends of internationalization and consolidation. Yet, evidence that the banks needed to be bigger to compete internationally was not particularly convincing. The MacKay Report pointed out that "A recent survey of the literature covering 23 different studies found that economies of scale do exist for small institutions with up to about $5 billion in assets, but that beyond this size it was difficult to find significant economies of scale or scope" (Canada, 1998a: 108). The MacKay Report was followed by hearings and reports by the Liberal Caucus, the House Finance Committee and the Senate Banking Committee. The former rejected the mergers outright, while the latter two supported MacKay's recommendation that mergers could be approved if, and only if, they were in the public interest.

...if one of the merged banks ever faced insolvency it would represent a huge challenge to regulators and the Canadian economy.

The Finance Minister rejected the proposed mergers in December 1998 on the grounds that they would lead to an unacceptable concentration of economic power, a significant reduction in competition and reduced policy flexibility for the government to address potential future prudential concerns. The Minister based his decision on the reports from the Competition Bureau and the OSFI. The Competition Bureau found that mergers would result in "a substantial lessening or prevention of competition that would cause higher prices and lower levels of service and choice for several key banking services in Canada" (Competition Bureau, 1998a and 1998b). The Superintendent of Financial Institutions suggested that if one of the merged banks ever faced insolvency it would represent a huge challenge to regulators and the Canadian economy (OSFI, 1998).

The Finance Minister was also well aware of the movement

against the mergers. The mergers faced strong opposition from such diverse quarters as Peter Godsoe, Chairman of the Bank of Nova Scotia, many non-bank financial institutions (including the life insurance companies), the Canadian Federation of Independent Business, the Retail Council of Canada, the Council of Canadians, the Canadian Community Reinvestment Coalition, the New Democratic Party and much of the Liberal caucus (Tickell, 2000: 166-167). To some degree the banks' position was hurt by lack of support from their natural allies (Whittington, 1999: 200). A survey conducted by the Conference Board of Canada (1998) suggested that corporate Canada did not favour bank mergers. The CBA and the Business Council on National Issues were weakened by the split in their ranks (Noble, Nicol and Hunter, 1998).

As he rejected the mergers, Paul Martin (1998) declared: "Whereas the merger proponents wanted the mergers to be allowed in order to change the status quo, we believe the status quo must be changed before any merger can be considered...The government will not consider any merger among major banks until the new policy framework is in place." Martin referred specifically to the demutualization of the major insurance companies and the removal of the ban on branches of foreign banks in Canada. Since 1998, the federal government has strived to alter the status quo to prepare the groundwork for bank mergers.

THE CANADIAN FINANCIAL SERVICES SECTOR TODAY: TRANSNATIONAL FINANCIAL GROUPS

"If we attempt to preserve the status quo – by not allowing the banks to merge – here is what I believe will happen. Over the next five years, Canadian banks will lose their competitive edge to larger, more efficient global competitors, particularly in our home market."

Al Flood, CIBC
1998

"I do think...the banks often do protest too much, because they seem to have done very well over the last number of years, despite their not being able to merge"

Catherine Swift, Canadian Federation of Independent Business
January 28, 2002.

Two Super Pillars and the Foreign Threat

Overall, the major Canadian banks have done very well through regulatory reform and have reaped record profits. After a weak year in 2002 in which the big six banks made only $7 billion, the banks rebounded with a record combined profit of $13.3 billion in fiscal 2004 (see Table 6). After the bank mergers were rejected by the Liberal government, the banks did not wither and die and the financial services sector did not stagnate. The regulatory environment did not stand still and neither have the financial firms. The profile of bank profits has changed significantly over the years. Serving as financial intermediaries coexists with wealth management, investment banking, derivatives trading and foreign currency exchange. With their merger plans blocked, the banks have pursued other opportunities. The most notable changes, however, have taken place in the life insurance sector.

In January 1999, less than two months after the bank mergers were rejected, officials from TD bank were meeting with the Department of Finance to discuss their plans to purchase Canada Trust (McIntosh, 1999). The deal worth $8 billion was announced publicly in

August 1999 and officially approved by the Finance Minister in January 2000. TD's takeover of Canada Trust generated relatively little controversy or attention, despite the significant size of Canada Trust.[7] At the time, the acquisition vaulted TD from being Canada's fifth-largest bank measured by assets to third place (De Cloet, 1999). Thus, the last remaining large independent trust was gone.

Table 6: Bank Profits (and Losses), 1998-2004
(in $ billions)

	1998	1999	2000	2001	2002	2003	2004
RBC	1.8	1.8	2.3	2.4	2.8	3.0	2.8
Scotiabank	1.4	1.6	2.0	2.2	1.8	2.5	2.9
CIBC	1.1	1.0	2.1	1.7	0.7	2.1	2.2
BMO	1.4	1.4	1.9	1.5	1.4	1.8	2.4
TD	1.1	3.0	1.0	1.4	(0.1)	1.1	2.3
National	0.3	0.4	0.5	0.6	0.4	0.6	0.7
Total	7.1	9.1	9.7	9.7	7.0	11.1	13.3

Source: Canadian Bankers Association, *Database of Domestic Banks Financial Results.*

Though the life insurance sector felt the impact of the dissolving of the pillars, a major restructuring of the insurance sector did not occur until after 1999 when the federal government passed legislation to permit large federally regulated mutually owned life insurance companies to convert into publicly listed shareholder owned companies, a process known as demutualization. This was intended to give them access to an important source of financing as well a giving them greater organizational flexibility. It would also facilitate consolidation in the insurance sector after a government mandated breathing period of two years during which no mergers or acquisitions of demutualized firms were allowed. The five largest mutual life insurance companies (Manulife, Sun Life, Canada Life, Mutual Life which renamed itself Clarica and Industrial-Alliance) then demutualized and issued shares in 1999-2000.

Shortly after the ban on mergers among the demutualized insurers ended, the life insurance sector witnessed a major wave of consolidations. In December 2001, Sun Life acquired Clarica (formerly Mutual Life) for $7.3 billion. In December 2002, Great-West Lifeco, part of the Power Corp. empire, struck a $7.3 billion deal to buy Canada Life. As described below, Manulife would strike the biggest deal through a foreign acquisition. Manulife, Great-West Life and Sun Life now dominate the domestic life insurance sector and rival the major banks in size. Manulife made $2.55 billion last year, a record profit for the Canadian insurance sector, and comparable to the profits of the big banks. Demutualization and the subsequent consolidation have strengthened the largest insurance companies as diversified financial groups and competitors to the banks.

The major banks argue that along with the domestic competition among themselves and from other financial institutions, they face increasing competition from foreign entrants to the Canadian market. However, this threat should not be exaggerated. Foreign banks have not launched an all-out assault on the Canadian market and remain relatively small in size (see Tables 7 and 8). The number of foreign bank subsidiaries in Canada peaked at 59 in 1987; at present there are only 27 (Canada, 1998b: 103; OSFI, 2005). In 2002, only 6.9 percent of the assets and 6.0 percent of the operating revenues within Canada's deposit credit intermediation sector (banking and credit unions) were foreign controlled (Statistics Canada, 2004: 23). According to Statistics Canada, "The dominance of the Canadian chartered banks and heavy government regulation in this industry continues to curtail foreign control of the financial sector" (2002: 11).

Jeffrey Orr,
CEO, Power Financial Corporation

Following the completion of a financial services agreement under the rubric of the WTO in December 1997, the federal government passed legislation allowing foreign branch banking in Canada in June of 1999 (Finance, 1999).[8] Two types of branches are allowed: a full-service branch or a lending branch. Even so-called full-service branches are not permitted to take retail deposits (defined as deposits under $150 000). Retail banking by foreign-owned banks remains the preserve of fully regulated Canadian subsidiaries.

Table 7: Canadian Banks
Ranked by Assets, 2004 ($ millions)

		Total Assets[2]
1	Royal Bank	429,196
2	TD Bank[1]	311,027
3	Bank of Nova Scotia	279,218
4	CIBC[2]	278,764
5	Bank of Montreal	265,194
6	National Bank	88,806
7	Laurentian Bank	16,607
8	Canadian Western Bank	4,919
9	Manulife Bank of Canada	3,636
10	Citizens Bank of Canada	1,585
11	Sears Bank	1,444
12	Pacific and Western Bank	1,004
13	Canadian Tire Bank	809
14	President's Choice Bank	145
15	CS Alterna Bank	103
16	Bank West	60
17	Ubiquity Bank	49
	Total Domestic Banks	1,682,561

As of October 31, 2004.
1. Includes the assets of the First Nations Bank of Canada.
2. Includes the assets of Amicus Bank

Source: Office of the Superintendent of Financial Institutions (OSFI).

Opportunities for foreign banks in the Canadian retail sector remain highly constrained. As Stephen Clarkson explains, "Their possibilities for expansion apparently remained limited because of the state's defensive and offensive measures on behalf of the chartered banks" (2002: 161). Defensive protection against foreign takeover continues to be offered by the widely held rule. In terms of an offensive strategy of reinforcing the banks, desegmentation allowed them to expand domestically and become dominant players across the financial services sector.

Table 8: Foreign Banks in Canada
Ranked by Assets, 2004 ($ millions)

Ten Largest Foreign Bank Subsidiaries in Canada

		Total Assets
1	HSBC	42,719
2	ING Bank of Canada	15,575
3	Citibank Canada	13,286
4	Société Générale	8,611
5	BNP Paribas	4,578
6	Amex Bank of Canada	3,537
7	Bank of Tokyo-Mitsibishi	2,153
8	MBNA Bank of Canada	1,623
9	Sumitomo Mitsui Banking Corporation	1,091
10	UBS Bank	653
	Total All Foreign Bank Subsidiaries	97,794

Ten Largest Foreign Bank Branches in Canada

		Total Assets
1	Citibank	7,454
2	Deutsche Bank	6,151
3	Bank of America	5,120
4	ABN AMRO Bank N.V.	2,991
5	JP Morgan Chase Bank	2,691
6	State Street	2,501
7	Bank One	1,155
8	Capital One Bank	1,145
9	Maple Bank	992
10	Radobank Nederland	963
	Total All Foreign Bank Branches	36,441

As of October 31, 2004.

Source: Office of the Superintendent of Financial Institutions (OSFI).

It is extremely unlikely that a foreign competitor could challenge the major Canadian banks in retail branch banking unless they were allowed to takeover an existing bank. British owned HSBC is the only foreign bank with a significant branch banking network, which it developed, in part, through taking over two small banks, the Bank of British Columbia and Lloyds Bank during the 1980s. Even without a branch network, consumer banking is not entirely immune to foreign competition. With much fanfare, ING Bank, a subsidiary of a huge Dutch financial services conglomerate has developed a 'virtual bank' in Canada specializing in higher interest rate savings accounts. The major banks fear that foreign competitors will focus on lucrative sections of the Canadian market. For example, MBNA, a huge American bank has aggressively entered the Canadian credit card market (Canada, 1998a: 49).

The greatest challenge from foreign competitors is in investment and corporate banking. The banks' role as supplier of large corporate loans has declined as a result of corporate access to international capital markets, securitization and the emergence of new suppliers of funds (Canada, 1998a: 64). According to the MacKay Report,

> *there is a clear trend for large businesses to look for their needs to many banking suppliers, and increasingly to foreign financial services providers, who are seen as more innovative and more capable internationally. The traditional relationships of large Canadian businesses with domestic banks have clearly been replaced with more discriminating and more critical ones (Canada, 1998a: 61).*

It is extremely unlikely that a foreign competitor could challenge the major Canadian banks in retail branch banking unless they were allowed to takeover an existing bank.

Foreign, primarily American, firms are playing a major role in underwriting international equity and debt issues for Canadian companies and advising on mergers and acquisitions (Canada, 1998b: 119; Willis, 2003). This represents a significant loss for the Canadian brokers as they miss out on the biggest and most lucrative deals. Their size, expertise and access to American capital markets make the largest American firms extremely tough competition for the Canadian brokers (IDA, 2005). Yet, even if they merged, the Canadian banks are unlikely to break into the first tier of global investment banks. As the MacKay Task Force suggested:

> *It is difficult to point to any forces at this time which would lead to the emergence of a Canadian global financial centre or Canadian financial companies as truly global institutions in investment banking and capital markets...the needs of Canadian corporate participants in global capital markets will probably continue to be met mainly by the large international service providers (Canada, 1998b: 120).*

Gordon Nixon,
CEO, RBC Financial Group

Still, the challenge facing Canada's capital markets should not be exaggerated. A recent study found little evidence "that domestic capital markets have been abandoned by Canadian firms or have been hollowed out" (Freedman and Engert, 2003: 15).

At the same time, new forms of corporate finance such as syndicated loans, securitized instruments and credit derivatives have become increasingly important (Freedman and Engert, 2003: 15). Without going into the technical details of these instruments, it is clear that the Canadians banks have been adapting to this changing financial market. The Canadian syndicated loan market developed in the 1990s allowing "Canadian borrowers...to rely relatively less on the US market" (Armstrong 2003: 29). The Canadian banks have also been involved in the US syndicated loan market for years. The Canadian market for asset-backed commercial paper (ABCP), the dominant form of securitization in this country emerged only in the late 1990s but was worth $63.7 billion at the end of 2002 (Toovey and Kiff, 2003: 43, 48). The major banks account for about 90 percent of the outstanding asset-backed commercial paper in Canada, with three of them (BMO, CIBC and TD) accounting for over 75 percent (Toovey and Kiff, 2003: 44).

To summarize, bank profits today are the result of a diverse range of economic activities. In general, the percentage of bank profits obtained through non-interest based activities has grown. In 2004, interest income accounted for only 46 percent of total bank profits for the big six banks (CBA, 2004b).

Continuing Regulatory Reform: Laying the Groundwork for Mergers

In this changing marketplace, the regulatory role of governments has continued to evolve. The trend of combining market liberalization with re-regulation continues. Following up the reforms to the OSFI and prudential overview in 1996, further steps were taken in 2001 to increase the OSFI's supervisory powers. These powers increase the consequences for any institution that fails to meet certain regulatory or supervisory requirements. The OSFI was given the power to remove directors and senior officers from office in certain circumstances, such as instances of misconduct.

...bank profits today are the result of a diverse range of economic activities.

In order to create common ownership regulations for both banks and demutualized insurance companies, a new size-based ownership regime was introduced by the federal government in 2001. Small financial institutions with equity under $1 billion have no obligation to be widely held. Medium-sized financial institutions with equity between $1 billion and $5 billion are allowed to be closely held with only a requirement of floating 35 percent of shares on the market. These provisions would allow a domestic or foreign commercial enterprise to purchase or establish a small or medium-sized bank.[9] Along with allowing small banks to be closely held, the federal government reduced the amount of capital needed to apply for a charter from $10 million to $5 million. These moves were designed to facilitate the creation of new financial institutions. The first new bank incorporated under the new ownership regulations, Bank West, a subsidiary of Western Financial Group, opened for business on January 30, 2003.

Other banks created under the new rules include Canadian Tire Bank and Sears Bank.[10] Along with the allowance for foreign bank branches, the reduced barriers to creating new banks has been portrayed by the federal government as increasing the competition within the Canadian banking sector. The state and the banks would like to use this as an argument to permit domestic mergers.

Other banks created under the new rules include Canadian Tire Bank and Sears Bank.

For the largest financial institutions, with over $5 billion in equity, the 10 percent ownership limit per single shareholder can be increased to 20 percent of voting shares and 30 percent of non-voting shares. Altering the 10 percent rule was intended to offer the banks greater flexibility to enter into joint ventures and strategic alliances with other firms (Schacter, 1999). Critics warn that "the move to 20 percent makes no intuitive sense… [and] raises the possibility of control while maintaining the fiction of being widely-held" (Peters and Peters, 2001: 509). The move to 20 percent opens the door for further changes in ownership rules.

In 2001 the federal government introduced new consumer protection legislation for the financial sector and created new institutions to oversee the new regulations and guidelines. Consumer and community protections provided through either legislation or guidelines include: guaranteed consumer access to a banking account with basic identification, access to basic low-cost banking services, the right to cash a government cheque without paying a fee, a requirement for annual public accountability statements by all financial institutions with equity above $1 billion, advance notice of branch closures and broadened coercive tied selling provisions.[11] A new federal agency, the Financial Consumer Agency of Canada (FCAC) was established in October 2001 to oversee consumer protection measures and promote consumer awareness. After promising to create an independent Canadian Financial Services Ombudsman the federal government backed off and supported the industry's own Financial Services OmbudsNetwork.

While the banking industry publicly protests against this array of regulations and guidelines, in effect the federal government has merely been forcing the major financial firms to develop their public relations skills under the guise of corporate responsibility. For example, by requiring banks to develop annual public accountability statements, the government has forced the banks to develop continuously updated public relations documents that can be used to demonstrate their social responsibility and good corporate citizenship. For its part the government can now try and argue that it has the prudential regulations and consumer protections in place to allow consolidation within the sector.

Heading South: Continental Expansion

The major Canadian banks and insurance companies are all active internationally and have long been an important source of Canadian direct foreign investment abroad (Burgess, 2000). In 2001, within the financial services sector, Canadian direct investment abroad was worth more than three times the value of foreign direct investment in Canada. Overall, Canadian direct investment abroad in financial services doubled between 1995 and 2001 as a percentage of Canada's GDP, while foreign direct investment in Canadian financial services remained constant (O'Neill, 2002: 23). It is notable that as they expand abroad, Canadian financial transnationals including RBC Financial Group, BMO Financial Group and Sun Life Financial Inc.[12] have followed Nortel Networks in rebranding themselves in a manner that erases their geographical references to Canada.

Tony Comper, CEO, BMO Financial Group

During the 1990s, four of the five major Canadian banks focused on North American strategies (Darroch, 1994; 1999). The Bank of Nova Scotia was the exception as it built on its traditional base in Latin America and the Caribbean. It continues to follow this pattern as exhibited by its acquisition in 2004 of the fourth largest bank in El Salvador. The other major Canadian banks focused their foreign strategies on the American market. The liberalization of the American banking sector to allow inter-state banking and the combination of commercial and investment banking has opened up opportunities for consolidation within the US. Led by the Royal Bank and the Bank of Montreal which have made numerous small acquisitions, the big five Canadian banks have purchased more than 30 US financial institutions since 1999 (Ouellette, 2004; See Table 9).

Table 9: BMO and RBC Acquisitions in the US.

BMO acquisitions in US

Year	Acquisition	Purchase Price (millions of Canadian $)
1984	Harris Bank	$718
1985	First National Bank of Barrington	$43
1987	Commercial State Bank (Phoenix)	$3
1988	State Bank of St. Charles and First National Bank of Batavia	$31
1990	Frankfort Bancshares	$20
1990	Libertyville Federal Savings & Loan	$7
1994	Suburban Bancorp	$300
1996	Household International	$378
1999	Burke, Christensen and Lewis	$59
2000	Century Bank	$24
2000	Freeman Welwood	$140
2000	Village Banc of Naplcs	$19
2001	First National Bank of Joliet	$337
2002	my CFO	$61
2002	Self-directed online client accounts of Morgan Stanley	$153
2002	Northwestern Trust	$19
2002	CFSB*direct*	$854
2003	Sullivan, Bruyette, Speros & Blayney	$20
2003	Gerard Klauer Mattison	$40
2004	Mercantile Bancorp	$197
2004	New Lenox State Bank	$314
2004	Lakeland Community Bank	$49

RBC acquisitions in US

Year	Acquisition	Purchase Price (millions of US$)
2000	Prism Financial Corp	$115
2000	Liberty Insurance	$580
2000	Dain Rauscher Corp	$1,456
2001	Centura Banks	$2,300
2001	Tucker Anthony Sutro	$625
2002	Eagle Bancshares	$153
2002	insurance and mutual fund	$220

The Bank of Montreal has slowly built up a base in the mid-western US centred around the Harris Bank of Chicago which it acquired in 1984. Since 2001, the Royal Bank has been developing an American retail banking presence in the south-eastern US through Centura Bank of North Carolina. In August 2004, TD announced its bid to purchase 51 percent of Banknorth Group Inc. for $5 billion. Based in Portland Maine, Banknorth has $29 billion (US) in assets and more than 350 branches in New England and upstate New York. In 2005, TD Banknorth purchased Hudson United Bancorp of New Jersey for $1.9 billion (US).

Despite all the bankers' talk about the expansion in the US, none have matched the splash made by Manulife's $15 billion takeover of Boston-based John Hancock Financial Services (including its Canadian subsidiary, Maritime Life). Through this deal Manulife became the largest publicly traded firm in Canada, the second largest life insurance company in North America and the fifth largest in the world measured by market capitalization (D'Alessandro, 2004: 6, 9).

Canadian bankers increasingly defend their goal of domestic consolidation with the argument that they need a larger capital base to expand abroad, particularly in the US. Ironically, foreign misadventures in recent years have played havoc with the Canadian banks' balance sheets. During the 2001-2002 financial crisis in Argentina, Scotiabank faced angry protests after it closed its subsidiary Scotiabank Quilmes. Ultimately, Scotiabank took a $540 million write-down and sold the subsidiary.

The US market in particular has presented as many challenges as opportunities for the Canadian banks in recent years. The meltdowns and scandals in the North American telecommunications and energy sectors rocked TD and CIBC. Problems in the US market, including the high-tech meltdown, led to a $2.9 billion loan-loss provision and an annual net loss for TD in fiscal 2002, a rare event indeed for one of Canada's major banks (Howlett, 2003). In response, TD slashed its corporate lending portfolio and restructured the international division of its discount brokerage and its US equity options trading business. In the same year, CIBC closed down its American electronic banking unit, known as Amicus, taking a $366 million write-down in the process, sold off its Oppenheimer brokerage and scaled down its US investment banking services (Stewart and Willis, 2004). While TD's purchase of Banknorth appears to be the first step in developing a regional retail banking presence in the US, the future strategy of CIBC in the US remains an open question. For now it appears to be focused on the domestic market.

Manulife became the largest publicly traded firm in Canada, the second largest life insurance company in North America and the fifth largest in the world measured by market capitalization

In 2004, it was the Royal Bank's turn to be pulled downward by difficulties with its American operations. RBC spent approximately $8 billion over four years to expand its American presence, but has had little return on its investment. In late 2004, RBC announced it would cut 1,600 jobs and RBC Centura has been forced to scale back expansion plans. The Royal Bank has been forced to restructure its US business to try and salvage its past investments (Laidlaw, 2005a).

Through their recent troubles in the US, the Canadian banks have been able to rely on their retail banking operations in Canada, which provide a steady source of income year after year. In the past the Canadian banks have complained that without mergers they lack the capital to aggressively expand in the US, but their recent problems managing their foreign acquisitions raises concerns about the potential instability and the domestic implications of larger excursions into the American market.

Too Many Fingers in Too Many Pies: Financial Scandals and Conflicts of Interest

The collapse of the stock market bubble and the bankruptcies of such previous high-flyers as Enron, Global Crossing, Adelphia and WorldCom produced stunning revelations about highly fraudulent business practices and dubious accounting procedures often perpetrated with the complicity of auditors and bankers. The intense pressure to boost short-term shareholder value and the prevalence of stock options as a method of executive compensation encouraged aggressive business practices and creative accounting. The banks were under similar pressure to make the big deals and sustain the stock market bubble. Looking at the American experience, former vice-president and chief economist of the World Bank Joseph Stiglitz has written that:

> *in the nineties, the banks became so eager for short-term profit that there was a race to the bottom. Each bank knew that its competitors were engaging in similar practices, and if it didn't compete, it would be left behind; and each banking officer knew what that meant: smaller bonuses, perhaps even being fired...The banks must surely have known that when the bubble burst, many of the loans that they had made would fail. Thus, the banks' loan portfolios depended on keeping the stock market bubble going (2003: 143-144).*

Thus, the Canadian banks should be seen as more than victims of others' corporate shenanigans. CIBC in particular was closely associated with two of the biggest bankruptcies in American history, Global Crossing and Enron.

CIBC's dealings with Global Crossing were very lucrative for the bank. CIBC managed to get in early, obtaining a 25 percent stake in the company in 1997. Then in 2000 it hedged its investments to ensure a healthy return. By the time Global Crossing filed for bankruptcy in early 2002, CIBC reportedly made a profit of $2.6 billion (US) on its investments in the company (McNish and Stewart, 2004).

In the infamous case of Enron, CIBC's ties with the company date back to 1991 (Howlett and Stewart, 2003). By the late 1990s CIBC was actively participating in deals which Enron used to manipulate its books. According to one account of the Enron scandal, CIBC "was falling over itself to please Enron" in order to become one of the energy firm's tier one banks (McLean and Elkind, 2003: 294). CIBC did join the inner circle of Enron's tier one banks in June 2000, but by the end of 2001 Enron had collapsed. In December 2003, CIBC struck an $80 million (US) settlement with the US Securities and Exchange Commission (SEC) for its role in the Enron debacle. The SEC accused CIBC of "having helped Enron to mislead its investors through a series of complex structured finance transactions over a period of several years preceding Enron's bankruptcy" (SEC, 2003). Then in August 2005, CIBC announced that it was paying $2.4 billion (US) to settle a class action suit launched by former Enron investors. This is the largest Enron-related settlement yet, larger than that paid by huge US banks like JP Morgan Chase and Citigroup. The Royal Bank and TD were also involved with Enron and have yet to reach settlements in the class action suit (Howlett and Waldie, 2003).

In December 2003, CIBC struck an $80 million (US) settlement with the US Securities and Exchange Commission (SEC) for its role in the Enron debacle.

A lower profile bankruptcy in the US also cost CIBC. In September 2003, a California jury ordered CIBC to pay $52 million (US) to money managers who claimed they were misled by the CIBC into buying bonds from Renaissance Cosmetics (Corman, 2003). In 1997 CIBC underwrote the cosmetics firm's bond issue, but the firm declared bankruptcy in 1999. In a classic example of a conflict of interest, CIBC was alleged to have misled investors about the status of the firm in order to recoup previous loans that the bank had made to that firm.

CIBC also found itself caught-up in the widespread mutual funds investigations in the United States. In February 2004, the former managing director at CIBC's New York office was charged with five felonies including grand larceny and securities fraud as part of an investigation into illegal mutual fund trading in the US (Ferguson, 2004). Another firm with Canadian ties was penalized as Sun Life's American subsidiary Massachusetts Financial Services reached two settlements with the SEC in 2004 involving over $US 400 million in fines and compensation for improper trading and other allegations (CBC, 2004).

This litany of foreign scandals should not be seen as implying that the Canadian marketplace is anymore honest or upstanding. If anything, US regulators have simply been more aggressive in their investigations. Canada has had its share of financial scandals from Bre-X to Nortel. CIBC, again in the middle of controversy, faced a number of lawsuits for its close relationship with Livent and its founder Garth Drabinsky, who still faces fraud charges in Canada and the US. The Canadian mutual fund industry came under increased scrutiny following the American revelations. Pushed into action by the American findings, the Ontario Securities Commission began conducting an investigation of potential trading abuses among mutual fund companies in November 2003. In December 2004, a record total of $203 million in penalties were assessed against seven of Canada's largest financial companies for improper trading practices (Westhead and Prashad, 2004). The OSC hit four of the biggest mutual fund companies with a total of $156.5 million in fines, these included AIC Ltd. ($58.8 million), CI Fund Management Inc. ($49.3 million), AGF Fund Management Ltd. ($29.2 million) and IG Investment Management Ltd. ($19.2 million). In a separate settlement with the Investment Dealers Association of Canada, TD Waterhouse agreed to pay $20.7 million, RBC Dominion Securities $16.9 million and BMO Nesbitt Burns $3.7 million. Additionally, Investors Group agreed to pay $5.3 million to the Mutual Fund Dealers Association of Canada. In the settlement, TD Waterhouse acknowledged that it had received and ignored eight written warnings from six mutual fund companies between 2002 and 2003 (Daw and Van Alphen, 2004). While the investigation and the penalties are a step forward, critics argue that improved

Edmund Clark,
CEO, TD Bank Financial Group

regulatory governance is required. After all, allegations of improper trading in Canada's mutual fund industry are not new. In 2000, RT Capital, then owned by the Royal Bank, was fined for manipulating stock prices and nine traders and officers of the company were disciplined (Blackwell, 2000).

Deregulation has broken down the barriers between commercial and investment banking and allowed financial institutions to engage in all kinds of new activities. This increases opportunities for conflicts of interests. According to Glorianne Stromberg, formerly of the Ontario Securities Commission, "it is hard to ignore the fact that the major financial institutions and conglomerates are trying to serve too many masters with the result that they are encountering conflicts wherever they turn" (2004: 8).

Banks and Insurance: A New Round of Mergers?

In 2001 the federal government introduced guidelines setting out a merger review process for banks with equity greater than $5 billion. In doing so, the government recognized that mergers were a feasible business decision. The process remains highly cumbersome from the perspective of the banks. The OSFI will review prudential concerns while the Competition Bureau reviews competitive concerns. The banks involved will be required to prepare a Public Interest Impact Assessment. The House of Commons Standing Committee on Finance and the Senate Standing Committee on Banking, Trade and Commerce are mandated to hold public hearings on specific mergers and report to the Minister of Finance on the broad public interest issues. Ultimate discretion for approving mergers remains in the hands of the Finance Minister. Supporters of bank mergers complain that the committee hearings and the ministerial discretion threaten to 'politicize' the process (Neufeld, 2001: 342).

In 2002, the bank merger issue resurfaced with rumoured negotiations between the Bank of Nova Scotia and the Bank of Montreal. Newspaper reports suggested that Finance Minister John Manley gave the banks encouraging signals before the Prime Minister's Office intervened to halt the merger (McNish and Partridge, 2002). In October 2002, Manley and Maurizio Bevilacqua, the Secretary of State responsible for International Financial Institutions, responded to bank concerns about ongoing uncertainty by asking for input from the House Finance Committee and the Senate Banking Committee to help clarify the public interest criteria involved in assessing big bank mergers.

The two committees held hearings and produced reports in late 2002 and early 2003. While supportive of mergers, the Senate committee recommended greater access to the Canadian market for foreign firms before allowing the Canadian banks to merge. The House committee was more cautious about both bank mergers and increased foreign competition in Canada, though neither was ruled out. In the hearings, a great deal of attention was paid to the possibility of bank-insurance company mergers. Before it acquired John Hancock, newspaper reports suggested that Manulife was interested in acquiring the CIBC (Reguly and McCarthy, 2003).

Richard Waugh, CEO, Scotiabank Group

There is immense pressure from the banks to allow mergers both between banks and between banks and insurance companies. Some critics of bank mergers would look more favourably upon allowing banks to merge with the insurance companies (Peters and Peters, 2001: 510-511; Olive, 2003). Allowing such mergers is seen as one way of facilitating greater size among Canadian financial institutions without reducing the number of banking competitors or bank branches. Manulife has publicly advocated that the government allow bank-insurance company mergers. The Canadian Bankers Association and all of the big banks have spoken out clearly in favour of allowing such mergers (2001: 16, 23). The Chair of the Senate Banking Committee came out in favour of permitting bank-insurance mergers (Kolber, 2003). On the other hand, Sun Life and Great-West Life have both made submissions to the federal government calling for a continued ban on cross-pillar mergers.

The banks took over the brokerage firms and the trusts, allowing further cross-pillar mergers would allow the banks to either takeover or merge with the life insurance firms. The international experience with such mergers is mixed, but that does not dull the enthusiasm of the CEOs, investment bankers and other advisors who see the short-term bonanzas to be gained through bonuses and stock options available through mergers. Allowing bank-insurance mergers would only make sense alongside the removal of the restriction against banks selling insurance in their branches. The branch distribution of insurance would increase the opportunities for the banks to engage in coercive tied selling: an individual with a mortgage or other bank loan would be under heightened pressure to also purchase insurance from that bank. The bottom line is that bank-insurance mergers would lead to a much greater concentration and centralization of financial assets and financial power within Canada.

In June 2003, the federal government responded to the Senate and House Committees on three points. As part of that response the government announced that it would seek further input on the issues of bank-insurance mergers and reduced barriers to foreign banks in Canada. Therefore, another round of industry and interest group submissions were submitted to the government by the end of 2003. The government promised to release its policies on these issues and revised merger review guidelines by June 30, 2004. With an impending election, these policies were soon delayed. Then the reduction of the Liberals to a minority government further postponed these guidelines. While the government avoids the topic, bank mergers have recently received the subtle and not-so-subtle support of Industry Minister David Emerson, Bank of Canada governor David Dodge and journalist Peter C. Newman among others.

John Hunkin, CEO, CIBC Retired as of August 1, 2005

While the Libcral minority government hesitates in the face of public opinion to give the banks a green light for any domestic mergers, it has taken some steps to try and pre-empt some of the concerns of merger opponents by encouraging greater competition and protecting consumer interests. As described above, the mandatory annual public accountability statements can be seen as a government-mandated public relations and self-promotion exercise for the financial institutions involved. The banks could help themselves by not tripping over their own feet. 2004 was not a great year in terms of public relations for

Canada's banks. In particular, CIBC appeared determined to set a new mark for corporate errors and apologies in late 2004.

In August 2004, CIBC reached a $16.5 million settlement (without admitting liability) with its Visa credit cardholders who had launched a class action suit against the bank over service charges related to foreign currency transactions. In November 2004, it was revealed that numerous CIBC branches had been faxing confidential customer information to the wrong number for three years (Akin, 2004). The story came to light after legal action was launched, not by a CIBC customer, but by the owner of a scrapyard in West Virginia who complained that all of CIBC's misdirected faxes had overwhelmed both his fax machine and his business! In fact, he apparently continued to receive CIBC faxes after he had complained to the bank in 2001 and after the fiasco made the front page of the Canadian newspapers in November 2004. No sooner had CIBC CEO John Hunkin apologized then one of his bank's ATMs in New Brunswick dispensed Canadian Tire money instead of $20 bills. Then in January 2005, over 3000 customers of President's Choice Financial, which is administered by CIBC, received improper tax reassessments from Canada Revenue Agency. The tax collector had incorrectly been told that these customers had cashed in part of their RRSPs in 2003 and issued the appropriate tax bills (Laidlaw, 2005b).

The bottom line is that bank-insurance mergers would lead to a much greater concentration and centralization of financial assets and financial power within Canada.

CIBC was apologizing again in February 2005 after another technical glitch resulted in their customers being unable to obtain their bank balances. That problem was quickly addressed and did not become a major headache, unlike the Royal Bank's computer problems the previous year. In June 2004, RBC had a massive computer malfunction, affecting payroll deposits and account balances for millions of customers. The chaos lasted for over a week and CEO Gord Nixon came under fire for leaving the country during the crisis (Saunders and

Pitts, 2004). Then in December, RBC was forced to refund more than 150,000 customers who had been overcharged when banking over the telephone and internet (Stewart, 2004).

While it was not directly under investigation, a pre-dawn raid on Scotiabank's Bay Street offices by the RCMP does little to inspire confidence. The raid was part of an on-going investigation into Royal Group Technologies, a building materials company and Scotiabank client. Scotiabank had been refusing to hand over documents demanded by the RCMP, citing solicitor-client confidentiality (Laidlaw and Ogilvie, 2005).

Canada's big banks face a major challenge trying to convince the public that bank mergers are in the public interest. The minority government in Ottawa is well aware of the political risks of allowing mergers. Along with the classic concerns about service charges, credit card interest rates and poor customer service, the banks' recent misadventures raise questions about corruption and incompetence.

CONCLUSION: 'BETTER BANKS, NOT BIGGER BANKS'

"You merge for only one reason, in my view. There is one overwhelming reason that can be given to the Canadian people, which is the overall scale of our equity base. Why do you need the size? It is to grow and expand outside of Canada faster. All of us are already generating excess capital, which forces us to go outside and look for acquisitions."

Peter Godsoe, Chair and CEO Scotiabank,
speaking to the Senate Banking Committee,
November 25, 2002.

"Martin told the banks to regroup, re-grease their public relations machinery, and then make him an offer he can't refuse...Martin is convinced that the "winning conditions" for a successful merger will include a significant deregulation of the financial sector, including opening up the Canadian market to more foreign banks. But more deregulation and foreign competition won't provide Canadians with better financial services. It's like offering us more poison instead of the antidote."

David Robinson, Canadian Centre for Policy Alternatives,
March 1999.

The Canadian banks reached their present size by being nurtured by the state. Canada's regulatory framework encouraged the emergence of large, stable, nation-wide banks. That size and strength has allowed them to absorb the other pillars domestically and expand internationally. The Canadian banks remain protected from foreign takeover by the widely held rule. The restrictions on the powers of foreign bank branches in Canada limit the growth of foreign banks in Canada.

The Canadian state may face foreign pressure to abandon (or further liberalize) the widely held rule in the name of reciprocity as Canadian banks continue to gobble up foreign firms (Mailander, 1999;

Whittington, 2003). As Scotiabank (2003) has told the federal government, "restrictive policies that protect the status quo will, over time, run counter to Canada's interest in the ongoing liberalization of foreign financial sector markets." Of course, when Scotiabank refers to 'Canada's interest' they are really referring to their own self-interest. It is the Canadian banks' interest in penetrating foreign markets that is at issue here. The six largest banks obtained approximately 33 percent of their net income from international activities in 2003 (CBA, 2004a: 2). They have come to realize that in order to expand abroad they must offer increased access to the Canadian market in return. Thus much of the pressure to open the Canadian financial sector comes from the domestic financial institutions.

The Canadian banks plan on appealing to Canadian nationalism and hope to sell mergers through flag-waving and warnings of foreign takeovers.

The debate within business circles is about timing, should bank mergers precede or follow a greater foreign banking presence in Canada, or should the two options be pursued simultaneously? Some vocal critics of bank mergers, such as the Canadian Federation of Independent Business and Hal Jackman, the Honourary Chairman of Empire Life and former Lieutenant Governor of Ontario, argue that Canada must first open itself further to foreign banks before considering mergers. The banks, not surprisingly, differ in opinion. For example, in early 2003, Edmund Clark President and CEO of the TD Bank, told the Finance Committee that "the logical order would be to resolve the domestic merger issues first, to allow our own financial institutions to gain in size where they can compete against larger foreign institutions...and then open the door to foreign entrants" (Canada, 2003). It is not at all clear how any of these developments, domestic bank mergers, increased foreign expansion by Canada's banks or increased foreign bank expansion in Canada, benefits the Canadian public. All of these developments grant greater powers to transnational financial firms, which they can then wield over governments, communities and workers.

The Canadian banks plan on appealing to Canadian nationalism and hope to sell mergers through flag-waving and warnings of foreign takeovers. The banks insist that the only way to preserve a financial sector characterized by Canadian firms with significant head office jobs in Canada is to allow them to grow bigger and stronger. Then our 'national champions' will have the size and strength to boldly take on foreign competitors here and abroad. However, there is nothing inevitable about opening up the Canadian market to foreign financial firms. It has been a conscious decision by successive Canadian governments, backed by the Canadian firms, to openly push for liberalization through the FTA, NAFTA, the WTO and the proposed Free Trade Area of the Americas.

The challenge for progressive Canadians is not to defend the market share of Canadian financial firms, it must be to gain democratic and collective control over the allocation of financial resources and redirect financial flows away from speculative adventures and towards investment in socially useful production. The Canadian Community Reinvestment Coalition sums up this goal as 'better banks, not bigger banks.' From this perspective, we can see that the real issue facing us is much broader than the prospect of mergers among the banks and/or the life insurance companies. Jim Stanford, an economist with the Canadian Autoworkers, has pointed out that the opposition to the bank mergers in 1998 often gave

> *the inadvertent impression...that a financial system dominated by three humungous, unaccountable, and super-profitable private institutions would be completely unacceptable, but that one dominated by five humungous, unaccountable, and super-profitable private institutions is quite acceptable (1999: 326).*

We must agree with the big banks, the status quo is not an option. Along with fighting against mergers, there must be a vision of a more democratic, more egalitarian, more sustainable, locally-controlled financial sector. The power of the financial elite and the power of international financial capital must be challenged.

Jim Stanford makes a number of provocative suggestions about how to do this including the creation of a new public investment bank and development councils set up on regional and sectoral lines to allocate resources (1999: 385-412). Up until the 1980s, some within the New Democratic Party were still debating one possibility, namely whether to nationalize one or more of the major chartered banks. The extent to which that is politically unthinkable today (in fact, many thought so back then!), demonstrates the degree to which the neo-liberal free market ideology has become entrenched and the left has been pushed entirely onto the defensive.

We must also address the internationalization of finance and continue to push for measures such as the Tobin tax on international financial transactions or more serious kinds of capital controls (Crotty and Epstein, 1996; Michalos, 1997). Restricting the power of international financial markets and building instruments to democratize investment is a necessary element of an alternative economic strategy based on social and ecological priorities (Albo, 1997). These ideas must be debated and further refined, but just as importantly a social and political movement needs to be built to make these projects more than just pipedreams.

The more immediate and modest goal is to struggle to make the existing private sector financial institutions more accountable to our collective needs while expanding the alternatives. If Canadians are concerned about preserving Canadian control over the financial services sector and want to restrict the ability of foreign financial giants to gobble up Canada than we should oppose further liberalization of the financial sector through the WTO and any changes to the widely-held ownership regime rather than allowing the banks to become even bigger. At the same time, Canadians should concern themselves with what Canada's roaming financial giants are doing in the US, Argentina, Mexico, China and elsewhere. We should not kid ourselves that Canadian-based transnational firms are more benign than any other kind.

To increase the accountability of financial institutions to local communities, we need to learn from the American experience with its Community Reinvestment Act as advocated by the Canadian Community Reinvestment Coalition (CCRC, 1997). The Community Reinvestment Act, which dates back to 1977, sets out a detailed disclosure and review system for American banks that rates their performance in lending, investment and service within their local community

(Squires, 2003). The act is far from perfect but it does create a higher degree of disclosure and accountability than exists in Canada. Such an act in Canada could be used to disclose and improve bank lending to disadvantaged groups and communities. As well, the Financial Consumer Agency of Canada should be strengthened to become a serious defender of the public interest and an advocate for public concerns. We must demand that regulators in Canada become more aggressive in tackling those firms that engage in improper trading and other dubious business practices. Too much of Canada's financial system remains poorly supervised by the government or under-supervised by guidelines and self-regulation.

The Community Reinvestment Act, which dates back to 1977, sets out a detailed disclosure and review system for American banks that rates their performance in lending, investment and service within their local community

Along with reigning in the big financial institutions we need to develop our own alternative institutions. Credit unions and caisses populaires have a long record of providing alternative financial services in Canada, but their strength varies widely across the country. Support should be given to expanding credit unions while preserving and improving their structure as democratic and member-controlled organizations.

Canada will soon be experiencing a revival of a public debate over bank mergers or bank-insurance mergers. This should be considered an opportunity to put wider issues about public accountability, democracy and local control of financial resources on the table. The banks fear this public debate and insist that the merger issue should not be 'politicized.' This time around, the banks will launch a more sophisticated public relations campaign to sell their mergers. It remains the task of community organizations, trade unions and other progressive organizations to politicize and challenge not just specific bank mergers but the very nature of corporate financial power itself.

Works Cited

Akin, David. 2004. "Internal faxes went to West Virginia for three years: CIBC's big gaffe." *Globe and Mail*. November 26.

Albo, Gregory. 1997. "A World Market of Opportunities? Capitalist Obstacles and Left Economic Policy." In Leo Panitch, ed., *The Socialist Register 1997: Ruthless Criticism of All that Exists*. Halifax: Fernwood.

Armstrong, Jim. 2003. *The Syndicated Loan Market: Developments in the North American Context*. Bank of Canada Working Paper. 2003-15, June.

Babad, Michael and Mulroney, Catherine. 1993. *Pillars: The Coming Crisis in Canada's Financial Industry*. Toronto: Stoddart.

Blackwell, Richard. 2000. "Royal Bank cleans house." *Globe and Mail*. July 21.

Bliss, Michael. 1987. *Northern Enterprise: Five Centuries of Canadian Business*. Toronto: McClelland and Stewart.

Burgess, Bill. 2000. "Foreign Direct Investment: Facts and Perceptions about Canada." *Canadian Geographer*. Vol. 44, No. 2.

Canada. Task force on the Future of the Canadian Financial Services Sector. 1998a. *Change, Challenge, Opportunity: Report of the Task Force*. September. Ottawa: Department of Finance.

Canada. Task force on the Future of the Canadian Financial Services Sector. 1998b. *Competition, Competitiveness and the Public Interest*. Background Paper #1. September. Ottawa: Department of Finance.

Canada. Task force on the Future of the Canadian Financial Services Sector. 1998c. *Organizational Flexibility for Financial Institutions: A Framework to Enhance Competition*. Background Paper #2. September. Ottawa: Department of Finance.

Canada. Parliament. Senate. Standing Committee on Banking, Trade and Commerce. 2002. *Evidence*. (Issue No. 7, November 27, 2002). 37th Parliament, 2nd Session. Ottawa: Public Works and Government Services Canada.

Canada. Parliament. House of Commons. Standing Committee on Finance. 2003. *Evidence*. (Issue No. 40, February 6, 2003). 37th Parliament, 2nd Session. Ottawa: Public Works and Government Services Canada.

Canadian Bankers Association (CBA). 2001. *Financial Services Reform 2001: The Canadian Bankers Association's Response to Bill C-8*. March.

Canadian Bankers Association (CBA). 2004a. *Bank Fast Facts 2004*.

Canadian Bankers Association (CBA). 2004b. *Database of Domestic Banks' Financial Results*.

Canadian Broadcasting Corporation (CBC). 2004. "Sun Life U.S. fund subsidiary pays $50 million US to settle SEC case." CBC.ca. March 31.

Canadian Business. 2004. "The Rich 100." *Canadian Business*. December 6.

Canadian Community Reinvestment Coalition (CCRC). 1997. *An Accountability System for Financial Institutions in Canada: How to Ensure They Meet a High Standard of Performance*. CCRC Position Paper #5. December.

Canadian Community Reinvestment Coalition (CCRC). 2000. *An Unjustifiable Takeover: A Performance Evaluation of Toronto-Dominion Bank and Canada Trust Based on the US Community Reinvestment Act Process*. CCRC Position Paper #9. March.

Canadian Life and Health Insurance Association (CLHIA). 2005. *Facts and Figures*. [www.clhia.ca].

Carroll, William K. 2004. *Corporate Power in a Globalizing World: A Study in Elite Social Organization*. Don Mills: Oxford University Press.

Chodos, Robert; Eric Hamovitch and Rae Murphy. 1998. *Paul Martin: A Political Biography*. Toronto: Lorimer.

Clarkson, Stephen. 2002. *Uncle Sam and Us: Globalization, Neoconservatism, and the Canadian State*. Toronto: University of Toronto Press.

Coleman, William D. 1996. *Financial Services, Globalization and Domestic Policy Change*. New York: St. Martin's Press.

Competition Bureau. 1998a. "Letter to the Royal Bank and the Bank of Montreal." [http://strategis.ic.gc.ca/SSG/ct01330e.html]. December 11.

Competition Bureau. 1998b. "Letter to the CIBC and the Toronto-Dominion Bank." [http://strategis.ic.gc.ca/SSG/ct01339e.html]. December 11.

Conference Board of Canada. 1998. *Corporate Banking Relationships in Canada: The CFO View*. Research Paper Prepared for the Task Force on the Future of the Canadian Financial Services Sector.

Corman, Linda. 2003. "CIBC: Exposed!" *US Credit*. Vol. 1, Issue 2. October.

Crotty, Jim and Gerald Epstein. 1996. "In Defence of Capital Controls." In Leo Panitch, ed., *The Socialist Register 1996: Are There Alternatives?* Halifax: Fernwood.

D'Alessandro, Dominic. 2004. *Charting our Destiny*. President's Annual Meeting Address. Manulife Financial. April 29.

Darroch, James L. 1994. *Canadian Banks and Global Competitiveness*. Montreal and Kingston: McGill-Queen's University Press.

Darroch, James L. 1999. "Canadian Banking Strategy in North America." In Jerry Haar and Krishnan Dandapani, ed., *Banking in North America: NAFTA and Beyond*. Oxford: Pergamon.

Daw, James and Tony Van Alphen. 2004. "TD Waterhouse ignored warnings." *Toronto Star*. December 17. E1.

De Cloet, Derek. 1999. "What's big, green and user friendly? By swallowing Canada Trust, TD's Charles Baillie may yet produce what passes for a miracle on Bay Street – the country's first consumer-savvy bank." *Canadian Business*. August 27. Vol. 72. No. 13.

Ferguson, Rob. 2004. "Ex-CIBC executive charged." *Toronto Star*. February 4.

Finance Department. 1999. "Foreign Bank Branching Legislation Comes Into Force." Press Release. June 28. Ottawa: Department of Finance.

Finance Department. 2002. *Canada's Life and Health Insurers*. [www.fin.gc.ca].

Freedman, Charles. 1998. *The Canadian Banking System*. Bank of Canada, Technical Report No. 81.

Freedman, Charles and Walter Engert. 2003. "Financial Developments in Canada: Past Trends and Future Challenges." *Bank of Canada Review*. Summer.

Helleiner, Eric. 1994. *States and the Reemergence of Global Finance: From Bretton Woods to the 1990s*. Ithaca: Cornell University Press.

Henwood, Doug. 2003. *After the New Economy*. New York: New Press.

Howlett, Karen. 2003. "How to break a nasty habit: TD Bank suffered a historic loss thanks to its co-dependency with addictive borrowers." *Canadian Business*. Vol. 19, No.7.

Howlett, Karen and Sinclair Stewart. 2003. "Roots run deep between Enron and CIBC." *Globe and Mail*. August 5.

Howlett, Karen and Paul Waldie. 2003. "RBC implicated over Enron." *Globe and Mail*. December 5.

Independent Investment Dealers (IID). 1997. *Submission to the Task Force on the Future of the Canadian Financial Services Sector*. March.

Investment Dealer Association of Canada (IDA). 2005. *Canada's M&A Activity: Heading South, Eh? An Overview of Canada's M&A Trends in 2004 and its Impact on the Canadian Securities Industry.*

Investment Funds Institute of Canada (IFIC). 2005. *Monthly Statistics – January 2005*.

Kolber, Leo. 2003. "Let Them Join, We'd All Be Richer." *Globe and Mail*. February 27.

Laidlaw, Stuart. 2005a. "Royal outlines plan to fix U.S. unit." *Toronto Star*. January 20.

Laidlaw, Stuart. 2005b. "Tax foul-up hits thousands." *Toronto Star*. January 26.

Laidlaw, Stuart and Megan Ogilvie. 2005. "How the Bay St. raid went down." *Toronto Star*. February 2.

MacIntosh, Robert. 1991. *Different Drummers: Banking and Politics in Canada*. Toronto: Macmillan.

Mailander, Christopher J. 1999. *Reshaping North American Banking: The Transforming Effects of Regional Market and Policy Shifts*. Policy Papers on the Americas. Vol. X, Study 5. Washington, DC: Center for Strategic and International Studies.

Martin, Paul. 1998. "Statement by The Honourable Paul Martin Minister of Finance on the bank merger proposals." December 14. Ottawa: Department of Finance.

McIntosh, Gord. 1999. "Ottawa informed on TD-Canada Trust." *Toronto Star*. December 4.

McLean, Bethany and Peter Elkind. 2003. *The Smartest Guys in the Room: The Amazing Rise and Scandalous Fall of Enron*. New York: Portfolio.

McNish, Jacquie and John Partridge. 2002. "Ottawa Kills Bank Merger Talks." *Globe and Mail*. October 29.

McNish, Jacquie and Sinclair Stewart. 2004. "CIBC repairs battered image." *Globe and Mail*. February 6.

McQueen, Rod. 1985. *Risky Business: Inside Canada's $86-Billion Insurance Industry*. Toronto: Macmillan.

Michalos, Alex C. 1997. *Good Taxes: The Case for Taxing Foreign Currency Exchange and Other Financial Transactions*. Toronto: Dundurn.

Nagy, P. 1983. *The International Business of Canadian Banks*. Montreal: Centre for International Business Studies.

Neufeld, Edward P. 2001. "Adjusting to Globalization: Challenges for the Canadian Banking System." In Patrick Grady and Andrew Sharpe, ed., *The State of Economics in Canada: Festschrift in Honour of David Slater*. Kingston & Montreal: McGill-Queen's University Press.

Newman, Peter C. 1998. *Titans: How the New Canadian Establishment Seized Power*. Toronto: Viking.

Noble, Kimberley; John Nicol and Jennifer Hunter. 1998. "How the Banks Blew It." *Maclean's*. December 7.

Office of the Superintendent of Financial Institutions (OSFI). 1998. "Proposed Mergers between the Royal Bank of Canada and the Bank of Montreal, and the Canadian Imperial Bank of Commerce and the Toronto-Dominion Bank: Report to the Minister of Finance." December 10. [www.fin.gc.ca/OSFI/osfirpt_e.html].

Office of the Superintendent of Financial Institutions (OSFI). 2005. "Who We Regulate." [http://www.osfi-bsif.gc.ca].

Olive, David. 2003. "Banks' merger pleas smack of amateurism." *Toronto Star*. February 28.

O'Neill, Tim. 2002. *North American Economic Integration...and Its Application to Canadian Banks*. Toronto: Bank of Montreal.

Ouellette, Gilles. 2004. "The Opportunities in a North America Without Borders." Presentation at the University of New Brunswick. March 9.

Peters, David W. and Douglas D. Peters. 2001. "Reforming Canada's Financial Services Sector – What Canada Needs to Follow from Bill C8." *Canadian Public Policy*. Vol. 27, No. 4.

Reguly, Eric and Shawn McCarthy. 2003. "Manulife Tried to Buy CIBC." *Globe and Mail*. January 14.

Saunders, John and Gordon Pitts. 2004. "Bank boss assailed for absence during crisis." *Globe and Mail*. June 9.

Schacter, Harvey. 1999. "Ottawa Unveils its Plans for Financial Services." *Canadian Banker*. July/August. Vol. 106, Issue 4. [www.canadianbanker.com/ past/JulyAug1999/eng/ottawa.htm].

Seccombe, Wally. 2000. "The Perverse Realities of 'Paper' in a Money-Driven Economy." *Studies in Political Economy*. 62.

Securities and Exchange Commission (SEC). 2003. *SEC Announces Agreement with Canadian Imperial Bank of Commerce and Two Executives to Settle Charges of Aiding and Abetting Enron Accounting Fraud*. Press Release. Washington, D.C. December 22.

Squires, Gregory D. (ed.) 2003. *Organizing Access to Capital: Advocacy and the Democratization of Financial Institutions*. Philadelphia: Temple University Press.

Stanford, Jim. 1999. *Paper Boom*. Toronto: Lorimer.

Statistics Canada. 2002. *Corporations Returns Act: 1999*. Catalogue no. 61-220-XIE. Ottawa: Minister of Industry.

Statistics Canada. 2004. *Corporations Returns Act: 2000*. Catalogue no. 61-220-XIE. Ottawa: Minister of Industry.

Stewart, Sinclair. 2004. "RBC clients get refund on charges." *Globe and Mail*. December 14.

Stewart, Sinclair and Andrew Willis. 2004. "Hunkin is 'de-risking the place.'" *Globe and Mail*. December 11.

Stiglitz, Joseph E. 2003. *The Roaring Nineties: A New History of the World's Most Prosperous Decade*. New York: W. W. Norton & Company.

Stromberg, Glorianne. 2004. *Submission to the Ontario Securities Commission on Proposed National Instrument 81-107*. April 9.

Tickell, Adam. 2000. "Global Rhetorics, National Politics: Pursuing Bank Mergers in Canada." *Antipode*. Vol. 32, No. 2.

Toovey, Paula and John Kiff. 2003. "Developments and Issues in the Canadian Market for Asset-Backed Commercial Paper" *Financial Systems Review*. Bank of Canada. June.

Waugh, Richard E. 2004. Presentation to Economic Club of Toronto. January 15.

Westhead, Rick and Sharda Prashad. 2004. "Financial sheriffs begin cleanup of 'Wild West." *Toronto Star*. December 17. E1.

White, William R. 1997. "International Agreements in the Area of Banking and Finance: Accomplishments and Outstanding Issues." In George M. von Furstenberg, ed., *Regulation and Supervision of Financial Institutions in the NAFTA Countries and Beyond.* Norwell, Mass: Kluwer Academic Publishers.

Whittington, Les. 1999. *The Banks: The Ongoing Battle for Control of Canada's Richest Business*. Toronto: Stoddart.

Whittington, Les. 2003. "Bankers Warn of Foreign-Buyout Risk." *Toronto Star*. February 4.

Willis, Andrew. 2003. "Glitz Sells: When there's a really big deal to be made, Wall Street's brand names are luring corporate Canada away from Bay Street." *Report on Business Magazine*. Vol. 19, No. 8. February.

Yakabuski, Konrad. 2004. "The Prime of Brian Mulroney." *Report on Business Magazine*. Volume 20, Number 11. May.

Endnotes

1 The banks primarily accepted deposits and extended commercial loans. Trust companies managed estates and trust funds, accepted short-term deposits and financed mortgages. Insurance companies underwrote insurance. The securities industry brokered the buying and selling of equities and underwrote new stock issues.

2 The Sobey family ranks 36th, Louie ranks 43rd, Sirois ranks 44th and Swartz ranks 48th. Nancy Southern is the daughter of Ron Southern who is 60th on the list.

3 The only Canadian Bank with a significant union presence is the seventh ranked Laurentian Bank.

4 Before 1992, the Bank Act was subject to review every ten years; it is now up for revision every five years.

5 Harold MacKay, the chair of the task force, has since become a director of the Toronto-Dominion Bank.

6 According to the MacKay Report, the auto manufacturers' finance companies lease about 70-80% of the cars leased in Canada. Auto dealers have about 10-15% of the market (Canada, 1998c: 100-101).

7 For one critique see (CCRC, 2000).

8 Some of the decline in the number of foreign bank subsidiaries in Canada can be attributed to foreign banks choosing to serve the Canadian market through branches rather than subsidiaries.

9 The existing smaller widely held banks (National Bank, Laurentian Bank and Canadian Western Bank) continue to be subject to the widely held rule. The Finance Minister has the discretion to approve requests to change that status.

10 Neither of these banks (Canadian Tire Bank and Sears Bank) accept retail deposits.

11 These reforms fall well short of the Canadian Community Reinvestment Coalition's desire for an American-style Community Reinvestment Act and the MacKay Report's recommendation for the creation of a Financial Consumers' Organization.

12 In 2003, Sun Life Financial Services of Canada Inc. was renamed Sun Life Financial Inc.